Martin Luther King Jr.

by Wil Mara

Content Consultant

Nanci R. Vargus, Ed.D.
Professor Emeritus, University of Indianapolis

Reading Consultant

Jeanne Clidas, Ph.D.

Children's Press®
An Imprint of Scholastic Inc.
New York Toronto London Auckland Sydney
Mexico City New Delhi Hong Kong
Danbury, Connecticut

Cataloging-in-Publication Data is available from the Library of Congress

ISBN 978-0-531-24738-9 (lib. bdg.)
ISBN 978-0-531-24704-4 (pbk.)

Produced by Spooky Cheetah Press
Poem by Jodie Shepherd

All rights reserved. Published in 2013 by Children's Press, an imprint of Scholastic Inc.

Printed in China 62

SCHOLASTIC, CHILDREN'S PRESS, ROOKIE BIOGRAPHIES®, and associated logos are trademarks and/or registered trademarks of Scholastic Inc.

1 2 3 4 5 6 7 8 9 10 R 22 21 20 19 18 17 16 15 14 13

Photographs © 2013: Alamy Images/Everett Collection Inc.: cover, 31 bottom; AP Images: 11 (Atlanta Journal-Constitution), 16 (Harold Valentine), 4, 30 left (Horace Cort), 20, 24, 27; Corbis Images: 12, 19, 23, 31 top, 31 center top (Bettmann), 15, 31 center bottom (Flip Schulke); Getty Images/Buyenlarge: 8; Polaris Images/Molly Riley: 28; Shutterstock, Inc.: 3 top (Neftali), 3 bottom, 30 right (Rudy Balasko).

Maps by XNR Productions, Inc.

Table of Contents

Meet Martin Luther King Jr.

Martin Luther King Jr. was a hero. He spent his life trying to end the unfair treatment of black people in America.

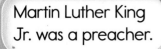

Martin Luther King Jr. was a preacher.

Martin was born on January 15, 1929, in Atlanta, Georgia. Like many African Americans at the time, Martin faced unfair treatment from white people. He was treated badly just because he had black skin.

Martin was born in Georgia.

Tennessee

MAP KEY

Georgia

★ City where Martin Luther King Jr. was born

South Carolina

★Atlanta

Georgia

Alabama

ATLANTIC OCEAN

Florida

Gulf of Mexico

In many places in America, black people were kept apart from white people. They could not go to the same schools or use the same bathrooms. Things that were meant for black people were not as good as those white people used.

An African-American child stands near a water fountain that is for black people only.

Martin was smart and worked hard. He did very well in school. While he was studying at Boston University, Martin met Coretta Scott. They were married in 1953 and later had four children: Yolanda, Martin Luther King III, Dexter, and Bernice.

A photo of Martin, his wife Coretta, and their children

A white woman tries to keep African Americans from eating at her restaurant.

Fighting Back

Martin wanted to change the bad way black people were treated. He thought they should be treated just as white people were.

Martin became a **pastor** in 1954. He talked to the people in his church about how they could fight for **equal rights**. Soon black people came from all over to hear Martin speak. They were tired of being treated unfairly. They asked Martin to help them.

FAST FACT!

Martin believed people should never hurt each other. He chose peaceful ways, like **marches**, to fight for change.

In Montgomery, Alabama, black people had to sit at the back of the bus. If there were not enough seats, they had to give up their seats to white riders. Martin told them to stop riding those buses. The bus companies lost a lot of money. Black people could sit anywhere they wished after that.

Martin was one of the first African Americans to ride a Montgomery bus after the seating laws were changed.

Martin also led many marches. People marched to let everyone know that they wanted unfair laws changed. A law is a rule that people have to follow.

Martin led many marches to try to change unfair laws.

Martin and other black leaders meet with President Johnson in the White House.

Giving His All

Martin also went to see President Lyndon Johnson. Martin asked the President to change laws that were unfair to African Americans. The President said he would.

President Johnson signs a law giving African Americans equal rights.

One of the new laws said stores, schools, and other places could not be for white people only. Another said black people could not be turned down for jobs just because of their skin color.

FAST FACT!

In 1963, Martin led a March on Washington for Jobs and Freedom. More than 200,000 people heard him give his famous "I Have a Dream" **speech**.

There were many white people who also wanted to help African Americans win equal rights.

Many white people thought Martin was right. They listened to his speeches and marched alongside him. Other white people hated Martin. They did not want him to win equal rights for black people.

One white person who hated Martin was James Earl Ray. He shot and killed Martin on April 4, 1968. James Earl Ray ran away after he shot Martin. But police finally caught him and put him in jail.

FAST FACT!

Every year we celebrate Martin Luther King Jr. day on the third Monday in January.

Martin stands on the balcony of a Tennessee motel on April 3, 1968. He was standing in the same spot when he was shot the next day.

Timeline of Martin Luther King Jr.'s Life

1954
becomes a pastor

1929
born on January 15

1955
organizes the Montgomery Bus Boycott

In 2011, a memorial honoring Martin Luther King Jr. was opened in Washington, D.C.

Martin Luther King Jr. is a very important person in American history. He will always be remembered for his fight for equal rights.

1963
gives his "I Have a Dream" speech

1968
dies on April 4

1964
President Johnson signs law granting equal rights

A Poem About Martin Luther King Jr.

Martin Luther King had a most amazing dream.

He worked his whole life long to make it true:

That people should be judged

not by the color of their skin,

but what they say and think and what they do.

You Can Make a Change

- Treat other people the way you want to be treated.

- Stand up for what you believe is right. If you see someone being treated unfairly, tell a grown-up.

30

Glossary

equal rights (EE-kwuhl rites): when the laws make sure everyone is allowed to do or have the same things

marches (march-es): when large groups of people walk together

pastor (PASS-tur): the head of a church

speech (speech): a talk given in front of a group of people

Index

Facts for Now

Visit this Scholastic Web site for more information on Martin Luther King Jr.:
www.factsfornow.scholastic.com
Enter the keywords **Martin Luther King Jr.**

About the Author

Wil Mara is the award-winning author of more than 140 books, many of which are educational titles for children.